AUSTRALIA

by Claire Vanden Branden

Cody Koala

An Imprint of Pop!
popbooksonline.com

abdobooks.com
Published by Pop!, a division of ABDO, PO Box 398166, Minneapolis, Minnesota 55439.

Printed in the United States of America, North Mankato, Minnesota.

082018
012019

THIS BOOK CONTAINS RECYCLED MATERIALS

Cover Photo: Shutterstock Images
Interior Photos: Shutterstock Images, 1, 5 (top), 5 (bottom left), 5 (bottom right), 6, 9, 11, 13 (top), 13 (bottom left), 13 (bottom right), 17, 20; Dave Watts/Biosphoto/Science Source, 14; Rick Rycroft/AP Images, 19

Editor: Charly Haley
Series Designer: Laura Mitchell

Library of Congress Control Number: 2018949679

Publisher's Cataloging-in-Publication Data
Names: Vanden Branden, Claire, author.
Title: Australia / by Claire Vanden Branden.
Description: Minneapolis, Minnesota: Pop!, 2019 | Series: Continents | Includes online resources and index.
Identifiers: ISBN 9781532161728 (lib. bdg.) | 9781641855433 (pbk) | ISBN 9781532162787 (ebook)
Subjects: LCSH: Australia--History--Juvenile literature. | Continents--Juvenile literature. | Geography--Juvenile literature.
Classification: DDC 919.4--dc23

Hello! My name is

Cody Koala

Pop open this book and you'll find QR codes like this one, loaded with information, so you can learn even more!

Scan this code* and others like it while you read, or visit the website below to make this book pop.

popbooksonline.com/australia

*Scanning QR codes requires a web-enabled smart device with a QR code reader app and a camera.

Table of Contents

Chapter 1

Australia

Australia is the smallest **continent** in the world. It is also a country. Australia is the only country that is also a continent.

Watch a video here!

MAP OF AUSTRALIA

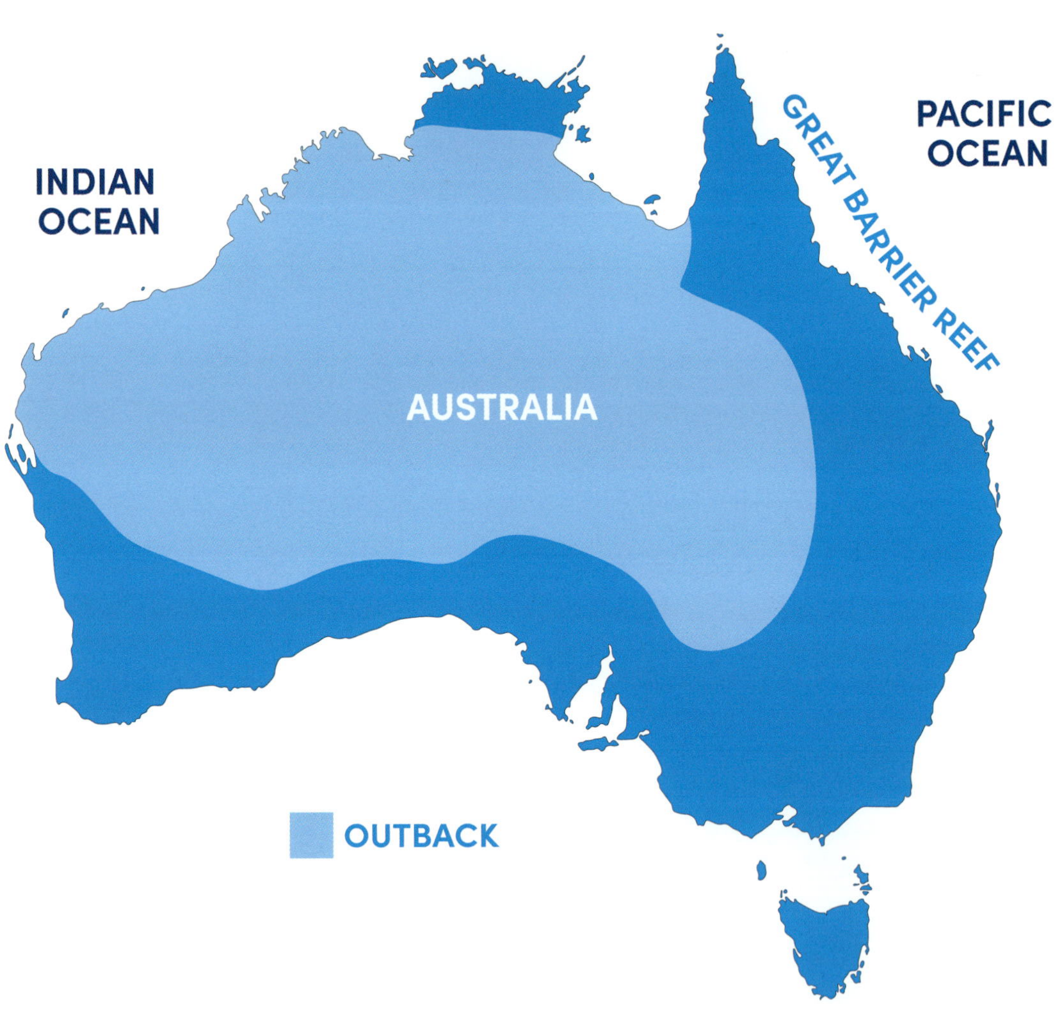

Australia touches the Indian Ocean and the Pacific Ocean. The continent is part of Oceania. Oceania is a group of many islands.

Australia is also called "the Land Down Under."

Chapter 2

Outback and Reef

Australia is hot. Most of the continent is made up of the Outback. This is a large **desert** where few people live.

emus in the Outback

Complete an activity here!

The Great Barrier **Reef** is on the northeast coast of Australia. It is the world's largest reef system. It can be seen from outer space!

There are many **rain forests** in Australia.

Chapter 3

Plants and Animals

Acacia and eucalyptus are common plants in Australia. But the continent has thousands of different kinds of plants. Many of the plants are poisonous.

Learn more here!

platypus

Australia has many animals that can only be found there. Koalas, kangaroos, and platypuses are only found in Australia.

There are many deadly animals in Australia. At least 20 kinds of **venomous** snakes and 36 kinds of dangerous spiders live there.

dangerous
taipan snake

Chapter 4

People of Australia

The **aboriginal people** of Australia have lived there for thousands of years. They were the first people to live in Australia.

Aboriginal people celebrate a traditional ceremony.

Now people from all over the world live in Australia. Some are from Europe. Others are from Asia. Each group keeps some of its **traditions**.

More than 24 million people live in Australia.

Making Connections

Text-to-Self

There are many different animals in Australia. Would you like to see any of them in real life? Which ones would you like to see?

Text-to-Text

Have you read another book about Australia? What did you learn?

Text-to-World

The aboriginal people of Australia lived there before anyone else. Why do you think it is important to learn about the aboriginal people?

Glossary

aboriginal people – the first people in an area.

continent – one of the seven large landmasses on Earth.

desert – a very dry area of land where it doesn't rain often.

rain forest – a tropical forest with many different plants and heavy rainfall.

reef – a group of rocks and coral in an ocean.

tradition – a belief or way of doing things that is passed down to different people over time.

venom – poison from an animal bite or sting.

Index

Online Resources

popbooksonline.com

Thanks for reading this Cody Koala book!

Scan this code* and others like it in this book, or visit the website below to make this book pop!

popbooksonline.com/australia

*Scanning QR codes requires a web-enabled smart device with a QR code reader app and a camera.